ZIMBABWE

A VISUAL SOUVENIR

Struik Publishers (Pty) Ltd
(a member of Struik New Holland Publishing
(Pty) Ltd)
80 McKenzie Street, Cape Town 8001
Reg. No.: 54/00965/07

ISBN 1 86872 209 0

First published in 1999

Copyright in published edition:
Struik Publishers (Pty) Ltd 1999
Copyright in text:
Struik Publishers (Pty) Ltd 1999
Copyright in photographs:
As credited opposite

Managing editor: Annlerie van Rooyen
Designer: Sonia de Villiers
Text: Glynne Newlands

Reproduction: Hirt & Carter Cape (Pty) Ltd
Printing: Tien Wah Press
(Pte)Limited, Singapore

2 4 6 8 10 9 7 5 3 1

FRONT COVER: Aerial view of Victoria Falls.
SPINE: Elephant feeding from a sausage tree.
BACK COVER: Carvings at a Lake Kariba viewpoint.
TITLE PAGE: Elephants at Mana Pools.
RIGHT: Cruise boat on the upper Zambezi River.

INTRODUCTION

The name Zimbabwe conjures up images of the majestic Victoria Falls and the beauty of Lake Kariba. But this lovely country is one of Southern Africa's most diverse, with much to offer the lover of wildlife and the great outdoors. Of its many national parks, Hwange is perhaps the best known, especially for the great herds of elephant that roam its plains. Game also abounds along Kariba's shores, at the unspoilt Eden of Mana Pools, and at Gonarezhou, the hot, dry Lowveld sanctuary. In contrast are the Eastern Highlands with its lush plantations, waterfalls and rugged mountain ranges. Boasting a grandeur of a different kind are the tumbled rock formations of the Matobo Hills, while the enigmatic ruins of Great Zimbabwe capture the soul of a country steeped in history and tradition.

LEFT Mosi-oa-Tunya, *'the smoke that thunders': an apt name indeed for the magnificent Victoria Falls.*

LEFT The elegant and timeless Victoria Falls Hotel first opened its doors in 1904.

OPPOSITE A leisurely sunset cruise on the Zambezi River above the Falls is a highlight for most visitors.

FOLLOWING PAGES For the more adventurous, white-water rafting on the Zambezi provides the ultimate in thrilling experiences.

RIGHT Completed in 1905, the railway bridge leading to Zambia is the venue for bunji-jumpers to plunge 111 metres (364 feet) into the gorge below.

FOLLOWING PAGES Dressed in fantastic costumes, traditional dancers, including the Makishi shown here, perform nightly at various venues in and around Victoria Falls town.

LEFT Local handwork, such as these beautifully carved giraffe, is for sale along the road leading to Victoria Falls.

RIGHT The giant baobab tree in Zambezi Drive boasts a girth of 60 metres (200 feet).

ABOVE Hwange National Park, one of Africa's most important wildlife sanctuaries, is home to large herds of Cape buffalo.

OPPOSITE Game-viewing platforms, strategically placed throughout the park, allow visitors to observe animals in their natural habitat.

PREVIOUS PAGES *The world's largest concentration of elephant occur at Hwange National Park. More than 17,000 of these enormous pachyderms roam the park's plains.*

OPPOSITE *Ivory Lodge's thatched tree houses provide visitors to Hwange with unusual and luxurious accommodation.*

ABOVE *Giraffe and zebra gather at Nyamandhlovu Pan near Main Camp.*

LEFT The distinctive saddle-billed stork is a
year-round resident of the park.
OPPOSITE Annual visitors to Hwange are flocks
of carmine bee-eaters which nest in colonies
along the riverbanks.
FOLLOWING PAGES LEFT Bulawayo's unusually
wide streets are graced by old colonial buildings
and, in season, striking flamboyant trees.
RIGHT Chipangali Wildlife Orphanage on the
outskirts of Bulawayo cares for injured and
orphaned animals, such as this young rhino.

LEFT A vast, brooding landscape of giant granite boulders makes up World's View in the Matobo National Park near Bulawayo.

ABOVE Brightly coloured rock lizards have made their home among the sun-warmed rocks of the Matobo Hills.

LEFT San people roamed the Matobos for thousands of years. An excellent example of their art can be seen at Nswatugi Cave in the Matobo National Park.

OPPOSITE Mzilikazi, founder of the Ndebele nation, likened the rounded domes of the amatobo, *or bald-headed hills, to those of his elderly counsellors.*

PREVIOUS PAGES *Zimbabwe, meaning 'houses of stone', was named after the impressive ruins of Great Zimbabwe, a World Heritage Site.* LEFT *The conical tower inside the Great Enclosure is reminiscent of a giant grain basket, symbol of abundance.*

LEFT The carved soapstone birds found at Great Zimbabwe have been adopted as the country's national symbol.

OPPOSITE Aloes bloom among the tumbled walls of the ruins, which were built without mortar in the 13th and 14th centuries.

RIGHT Lake Mutirikwi near Masvingo forms part of a recreational park where fishing, sailing and game-viewing are on offer.

OPPOSITE Gonarezhou National Park in the Lowveld is famed for its strangely attractive baobab trees.

LEFT The hardy yet radiant Sabi Star, otherwise known as the impala lily, is another familiar Lowveld resident.

FOLLOWING PAGES Gonarezhou, meaning 'place of elephants', is home to more than 6,000 of these giant mammals (left), and to the dramatically sculpted Chilojo Cliffs (right).

LEFT The rugged Chimanimani mountain range in the Eastern Highlands is a paradise for ardent hikers.

OPPOSITE Chimanimani's Bridal Veil Falls tumble gracefully into the pool below.

LEFT *Tea plantations flourish in the lush and fertile Honde Valley.*
FOLLOWING PAGES *Tea pickers harvest the abundant crops of the Aberfoyle plantations.*

ABOVE Beautifully situated Leopard Rock is one of the Bvumba's more luxurious accommodation options.

OPPOSITE The gardens of La Rochelle in the Imbeza Valley are a mass of flowers, including rare orchids, and trees and shrubs.

RIGHT Grand views unfurl from World's View at Nyanga in the Eastern Highlands.

OPPOSITE Harare, the capital of Zimbabwe, is a lively, modern city with a distinctive African feel.

ABOVE Flower sellers add colour and character to the city's streets. This flower stall is situated close to Africa Unity Square.

RIGHT Heroes' Acre in Harare is a proud monument to the liberation struggle.
OPPOSITE Exciting Shona sculptures are displayed in a natural setting at Chapungu Kraal on Harare's outskirts.

RIGHT One of Southern Africa's most unspoilt wilderness areas, Mana Pools National Park can be explored on foot or by a more restful option, canoe.

FOLLOWING PAGES In the wet season, numerous elephant, and other animals, luxuriate in the lush floodplains of the Zambezi Valley.

PREVIOUS PAGES *Mana Pools is rich in wildlife, including the endangered wild dog (left) and huge numbers of buffalo (right).*
LEFT *The park's riverine forests are home to scores of plains zebra.*
FOLLOWING PAGES *Sunset gilds the drowned forest of Lake Kariba.*

LEFT A boat safari in the Matusadona National Park is the ideal way to view game along the lakeshore.

ABOVE The ultimate way to experience Lake Kariba is to hire a houseboat and enjoy fishing and game-viewing at your leisure.

ABOVE *Pods of hippo are a familiar sight to lake visitors.*
RIGHT *Kariba's crocodile farm breeds these prehistoric reptiles for commercial and restocking purposes.*

FOLLOWING PAGES *Two of the big cats found in Matusadona National Park are leopard (left) and lion (right). Both form part of the 'Big Five', the other animals being elephant, buffalo and rhino.*

PREVIOUS PAGES *Buffalo browse along the shores of Fothergill Island.*

LEFT *Evening is the time for the rigs to set sail for a night of productive kapenta fishing.*

FOLLOWING PAGES *Rural scenes such as this one are typically seen in the Ume River Valley near Lake Kariba.*

ENDPAPERS *Details of the stonework at the Great Zimbabwe ruins.*